Snap books®

Miley Ray Cyrus

by Heather E. Schwartz

☆☆☆☆

Capstone press®

Mankato, Minnesota

Snap Books are published by Capstone Press,
151 Good Counsel Drive, P.O. Box 669, Mankato, Minnesota 56002.
www.capstonepub.com

032010
005738R

Books published by Capstone Press are manufactured with paper
containing at least 10 percent post-consumer waste.

Library of Congress Cataloging-in-Publication Data
Schwartz, Heather E.
　　Miley Ray Cyrus / by Heather E. Schwartz.
　　p. cm. — (Snap books. Star biographies)
　　Includes bibliographical references and index.
　　Summary: "Describes the life and career of Miley Ray Cyrus" — Provided by publisher.
　　ISBN 978-1-4296-3398-7 (library binding)
　　1. Cyrus, Miley, 1992 — Juvenile literature. 2. Singers — United States — Biography — Juvenile literature.
3. Television actors and actresses — United States — Biography — Juvenile literature. I. Title. II. Series.
ML3930.C98S39 2010
782.42164092 — dc22　　　　　　　　　　　　　　　　　　　　　　　2009002746

Editor: Megan Peterson
Designer: Juliette Peters
Media Researcher: Marcie Spence

Photo Credits:
Alamy/Allstar Picture Library, 13; AP Images/Chris Pizzello, cover, 6; AP Images/Jason DeCrow, 24; Corbis/Andrew
Mills/Star Ledger, 19; Corbis Outline/Derrick Hood Photography, 10; Disney Channel/The Kobal Collection/Cohen,
Byron J., 15; Getty Images Inc./Eric Charbonneau/Le Studio/Wireimage, 20; Getty Images Inc./Frederick M. Brown,
5; Getty Images Inc./Gregg DeGuire/WireImage, 11; Getty Images Inc./Jon Kopaloff/FilmMagic, 27; Getty Images Inc./
Peter Bass/Wire Images, 23; Getty Images Inc./Ron Gallela, Ltd., 9; Getty Images Inc./Stephen Shugerman, 16; Getty
Images Inc./Vince Bucci, 7; Landov LLC/RAY STUBBLEBINE/Reuters, 29; Supplied by Capital Pictures, 17

Essential content terms are **bold** and are defined at the bottom of the page where they first appear.

Table of Contents

CHAPTER 1

Miley's Big Moment

On a chilly night in January 2008, thousands of tween girls crowded near the El Capitan Theatre in Los Angeles, California. They cheered when the Jonas Brothers arrived on the scene. They called out to Ashley Tisdale as she signed autographs on the red carpet. But the main attraction was a teen star with a huge smile and long, chocolate-colored curls.

The crowd's cheers erupted into screams when Miley Ray Cyrus stepped onto the red carpet. Miley was thrilled to see so many fans, friends, and family members. They had come for the movie **premiere** of *Hannah Montana & Miley Cyrus: Best of Both Worlds Concert*.

"It's awesome! To have all the celebrities here — they're all here for you! I'm so excited."
— Miley at the premiere of her film, from an interview with *MTV*.

premiere — the first public showing of a film

Miley debuted her newly darkened hair at the 2008 premiere of her movie.

Miley sparkled in a silver minidress with chiffon panels crossed in front. She carried a black satin clutch purse with a rhinestone **brooch**. She turned, posed, and flashed the peace sign for photographers. She chatted with reporters from *Extra*, *E!*, and other entertainment shows. She gushed about the after party. She told one reporter that even though her mother might not know it, she planned to stay out late!

Miley wasn't too surprised to find herself in the center of a star-studded event. At age 15, Miley was already a television star and singing sensation. She was possibly the most famous teen performer in the world.

Kevin, Joe, and Nick (left to right) of the Jonas Brothers costarred with Miley in the film.

brooch — a piece of jewelry that can be pinned to fabric

Oscar Glamour

When Miley was 15, she was invited to introduce a musical performance at the 2008 Academy Awards. She turned to top designers for a look worthy of the red carpet.

Miley impressed the **media** with her choice of a floor-length red chiffon gown designed by Valentino. Miley accessorized with dark red chandelier earrings in garnet, diamond, and gold by designer Neil Lane. She wore a low curly ponytail. Miley completed her outfit with a Mary Norton-designed bronze lizard clutch decorated with Swarovski crystals. The teen queen's look was elegant, classy, and sophisticated.

Miley was excited to walk the red carpet at the 2008 Academy Awards.

media — TV, radio, newspapers, and other communication forms that send out messages to large groups of people

Born to Perform

On November 23, 1992, Destiny Hope Cyrus was born in Franklin, Tennessee. As a baby, she had a sunny **disposition** and always smiled. Country singing star Billy Ray Cyrus gave his daughter the nickname "Smiley Miley." He eventually shortened it to Miley. The nickname stuck.

Miley grew up on a 500-acre ranch in Nashville, Tennessee. Her family also includes mom, Tish, older siblings Brandi, Trace, and Chris, and younger siblings Braison and Noah. The Cyrus family also has many furry and feathery members. They have four dogs, Fluke, Roadie, Shooter, and Tex. Rounding out the group are a lovebird named Zazu, a rabbit called Jack, and Miley's horse, Memphis.

disposition — a person's general attitude

Miley, shown here at age 2, often traveled with her dad when he was on tour.

Miley, shown here at age 9, enjoyed entertaining her family and friends from a young age.

School Days

Miley attended a public elementary school through the sixth grade. Even though she was good with numbers, Miley didn't like math. But she did enjoy reading and creative writing. Miley tried team sports but preferred cheerleading. She joined the Premier Tennessee All Stars cheerleading squad. Miley and the squad competed around the country and won several trophies.

The Acting Bug

Miley got the itch to perform by watching her famous father. Billy Ray Cyrus was a major country star in the 1990s. He released his hit song "Achy Breaky Heart" the same year Miley was born. When Billy Ray toured, Miley liked to tag along. She often ran on stage to sing with her dad. Billy Ray gave a 7-year-old Miley her first guitar at one of his fan club parties.

Trace, Tish, Brandi, and Billy Ray (left to right) joined Miley at the DVD release of *Hannah Montana: Pop Star Profile*.

When Miley decided to learn more about performing, her parents were worried. They asked her to wait until she was older to start her career. Miley couldn't wait. She took acting and singing lessons. Her vocal teacher also coached the Dixie Chicks, Carrie Underwood, and Christina Aguilera. Miley soon began **auditioning** for acting roles. When Miley was 8, she landed a role on her father's TV series *Doc*. Miley appeared in just two episodes. But she had several lines to memorize.

In 2003, Miley played a small part in the Tim Burton movie *Big Fish*. She had a few lines and was on screen for about five minutes. Winning a movie role was a major accomplishment for Miley. Acting was fun, and Miley wanted to do more.

The year 2003 also marked another milestone in Miley's life — she began the sixth grade. But Miley's school life soon turned ugly. A group of girls bullied Miley. They pushed her against lockers. They made fun of Miley's dad, calling him a one-hit wonder. Once, they even locked Miley in the bathroom. To feel better, Miley focused on acting and cheerleading.

audition — to try out for an acting role

Miley's Real Name

A few months after her 15th birthday, Miley legally changed her name from Destiny Hope Cyrus to Miley Ray Cyrus. She wanted her legal name to be the name she's always been called. Adding Ray was a tribute to her dad.

Miley isn't just popular as a person these days. Even her name is well-known and well-liked. In 2007, the name Miley made it on the list of most popular U.S. baby names for the very first time.

Miley's parents named her Destiny Hope because they believed it was her destiny to bring hope to the world.

CHAPTER 3

A Rising Star

Miley was at home in Tennessee when her **agent** told her about a casting call for a new Disney show, *Hannah Montana*. Miley liked the show's story of a young girl who is secretly a pop star. But Tennessee was far from the Hollywood studio where Disney planned to film. Miley refused let a little distance stop her from chasing her dream. She sent an audition tape to California.

Miley was only 11 years old when she sent her audition tape. The show's producers thought she was too small and too young. They turned her down for the show. But Miley wasn't willing to quit. She sent in more audition tapes. Finally producers invited her to Los Angeles to audition in person. Miley memorized lines from the show's script. She acted out different roles to prove what she could do. At first she aimed to win the part of Lilly, Hannah Montana's best friend. Eventually she started trying for the lead role.

agent — someone who helps actors find work

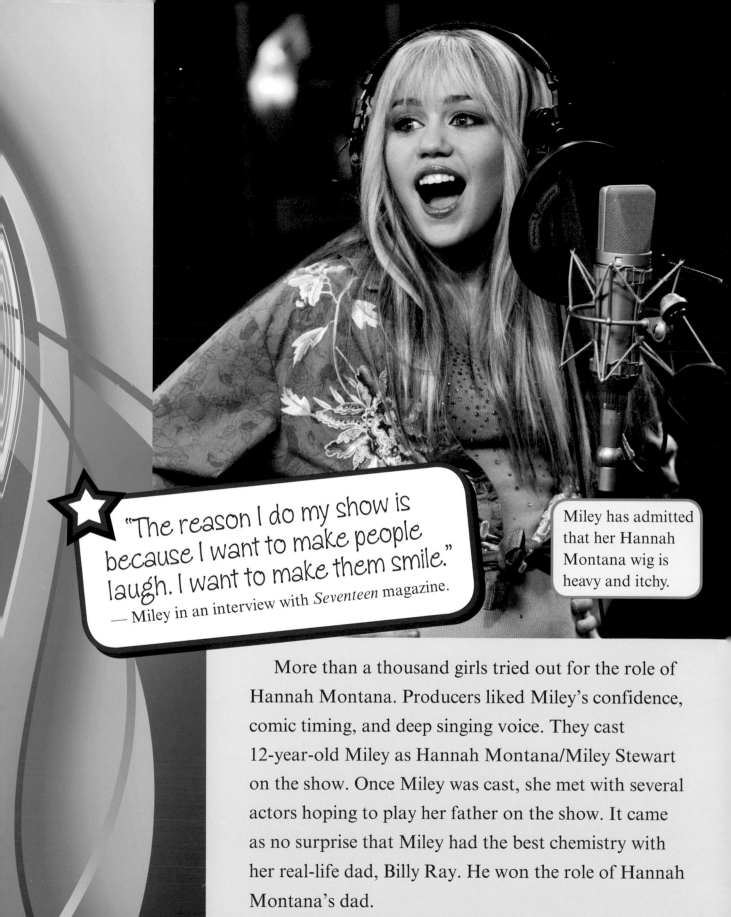

"The reason I do my show is because I want to make people laugh. I want to make them smile."
— Miley in an interview with *Seventeen* magazine.

Miley has admitted that her Hannah Montana wig is heavy and itchy.

More than a thousand girls tried out for the role of Hannah Montana. Producers liked Miley's confidence, comic timing, and deep singing voice. They cast 12-year-old Miley as Hannah Montana/Miley Stewart on the show. Once Miley was cast, she met with several actors hoping to play her father on the show. It came as no surprise that Miley had the best chemistry with her real-life dad, Billy Ray. He won the role of Hannah Montana's dad.

Miley, pictured with her *Hannah Montana* costar Jason Earles, enjoys meeting her fans.

TV Superstar

When *Hannah Montana* debuted on the Disney Channel in March 2006, 5.4 million people tuned in. Viewers quickly made *Hannah Montana* one of the most-watched cable shows for kids. Not long after the debut, fans recognized Miley while she was at an amusement park. Suddenly she was famous.

Nearly overnight, Miley went from the girl known as Billy Ray Cyrus's daughter to teen celebrity. Her family kept their ranch in Tennessee and bought a second home in California. The whole family moved to Toluca Lake, California, so Miley could do her job. But leaving Tennessee wasn't easy. Miley left behind friends and her favorite activity, cheerleading.

On the Set

Starting a career as an actress didn't leave Miley with much free time. *Hannah Montana* filmed Monday through Friday. Miley no longer attended regular school. Instead she worked with an on-set tutor for three hours each day. She sometimes squeezed school in between takes.

Miley became fast friends with costar Mitchel Musso, who plays Oliver on the show. But she didn't have the same instant bond with costar Emily Osment, who plays Lilly. Over time, they grew to be good friends. Miley, Emily, and Mitchel liked to hang out between takes and send each other silly text messages. Miley also spent a lot more time with her dad. Billy Ray was often away on tour when Miley was younger. She enjoyed the chance to make up for lost time.

Miley's *Hannah Montana* costar Emily Osment has a famous older brother. Haley Joel Osment has starred in *The Sixth Sense* and other films.

CHAPTER 4

Tapping Her Talents

Starring in *Hannah Montana* led to many more opportunities for Miley. During her first year in the role, she wrote songs that were used on the show. She also recorded a soundtrack album called *Hannah Montana*. To promote the album, Miley went on a 20-city tour with The Cheetah Girls, a band formed on a Disney show.

Best of Both Worlds

In June 2007, Miley released another album, *Hannah Montana 2/Meet Miley Cyrus*. She sang half the songs as Hannah and half as herself. She also headlined her own tour, Hannah Montana & Miley Cyrus: Best of Both Worlds Concert. Some shows sold out in as little as four minutes! Miley practiced with her band and dancers for several weeks leading up to the first concert. *High School Musical* alum Kenny Ortega directed the massive stage show. He was impressed by Miley's focus and sense of fun.

Before each show, Miley warmed up her voice while being fitted for her Hannah Montana wig. Once she took the stage, Miley rocked her fans with hit songs, complex dance numbers, and even a few fireworks.

During the Best of Both Worlds tour, Miley had several costume changes.

Miley also showed her audience a more personal side. She strummed her guitar for the song "I Miss You." She wrote the song in memory of her grandfather. Billy Ray joined Miley on stage for a duet of their song "Ready, Set, Don't Go." The same concert tour was later turned into a 3-D movie.

Life on the Road

Normal life didn't stop once Miley's tour bus hit the road. She was still tutored for three hours each day. For fun, Miley played video games with her sisters and jammed on her guitar. Miley's mom is her manager. Tish made sure Miley got plenty of sleep and woke up on time each morning. When not at a hotel, the family slept on tiny bunk beds on the bus. A Hello Kitty blanket covered Miley's bunk.

Life on the road was nothing new for the musical family. Miley's brother Trace is also a musician. He plays guitar and sings in the band Metro Station. Miley's sister Brandi plays backup guitar at some of Miley's concerts.

Miley cowrote one of the songs for *Bolt*. "I Thought I Lost You" was nominated for Best Original Song at the 2009 Golden Globe Awards.

Miley attended the premiere of *Hannah Montana: The Movie* with Billy Ray, Noah, Tish, Brandi, Braison, and Trace (left to right).

The Big Screen

Soon after the tour ended, Miley went to work on an animated Disney movie called *Bolt*. She voiced the character of Penny, a TV action star who loses her canine costar. She also started work on her second film, playing a familiar role. Miley and her family arranged to shoot *Hannah Montana: The Movie* in Los Angeles and Tennessee. They wanted to spend time on their Nashville farm. Miley spent the previous few months performing all over the country. She was happy to spend time at the home where she grew up. Excited fans flocked to the film when it hit theaters in April 2009. The movie debuted in first place and made $34 million opening weekend.

Going Solo

For her next album, Miley wanted to break away from her Hannah Montana identity. While on the Best of Both Worlds tour, she started writing new songs. Miley drew inspiration from the cities she visited and from her personal life. She wrote eight of the album's 13 songs.

Breakout debuted at number one on the Billboard 200 albums chart in July 2008. Miley wrote her favorite song, "7 Things," about her relationship with Nick Jonas of the Jonas Brothers. Fan sites spread the news that Miley wore a necklace he gave her in the song's video. Miley wasn't talking. But she did admit that the album showcased her flawed singing style. That was fine with Miley, who said **imperfection** was a theme of the album. To date, *Breakout* has sold more than 1 million copies.

"I write from life experiences — everything from guys to books I read that are inspiring to me. Someone will say something and I'll think, 'That'll be a great song title.' I just take a little bit of everything."
— Miley on how she writes her songs, from an interview with *Seventeen* magazine.

imperfection — the quality of being faulty or not perfect

Miley, shown in Berlin, Germany, traveled the world to promote *Breakout*.

Miley gets the chance to meet her celebrity idols, including Fergie.

Time Out

Miley doesn't like to talk about work when at home with her family. Instead she plays video games, swims, and gives her sister Noah makeovers. She also likes to ride bikes with her brother Braison. Miley and Billy Ray often go horseback riding together. Miley also enjoys going for coffee and shopping with friends who knew her before she became famous. They help ease the pressure Miley feels trying to be a good role model for her fans.

The Ups and Downs of Fame

Miley experienced the downside of fame when she posed for the magazine *Vanity Fair* in April 2008. Some fans thought the photos were too revealing. Miley apologized, explaining that she's not perfect and sometimes makes mistakes.

Wherever she goes, Miley is rarely alone. Photographers follow her to coffee shops and malls. They even follow her on family bike trips.

But Miley's life is also full of pop-star perks. She gets to attend star-studded events. She even meets other celebrities she admires, like Hilary Duff and Fergie. At the 2008 Academy Awards, Miley walked the red carpet alongside stars like Cameron Diaz and John Travolta. All the while, she rakes in the bucks doing what she loves most — acting and singing. Miley is expected to be a billionaire by the time she turns 18.

CHAPTER 5

Hannah Montana Grows Up

How does a girl who has it all celebrate her sweet 16 birthday? Miley hosted a party at Disneyland in California and invited fans to join the celebration. At $250 per ticket, admission to the birthday bash wasn't cheap. But Miley had a good reason to charge guests at her party. Disney donated $1 million to Youth Service America in Miley's honor. This organization gets young people involved in their communities as volunteers.

Miley's birthday party wasn't the first time she got involved in charity work. Throughout her Best of Both Worlds tour, Miley visited kids at children's hospitals. She also donated $1 from every ticket sold to City of Hope. This organization helps fight life-threatening diseases. Miley even helped out with a *Bolt*-inspired fund-raiser for the American Society for the Prevention of Cruelty to Animals.

Miley walked the purple carpet before kicking off her sweet 16 birthday party at Disneyland.

Future Plans

In the fall of 2008, the third season of *Hannah Montana* began filming. Miley still enjoyed playing Hannah. But she also wanted to try more complicated roles in independent films. She hoped to show the world her edgier, more grown-up side.

Miley will soon have the chance to sharpen her acting skills. She was asked to star in a movie based on the Nicholas Sparks novel *The Last Song*. The book and movie role were written specifically for Miley. She hopes the film will help her make the transition from teen pop star to adult actress.

Home Suite Home

Miley has a full-time career and her own steady paycheck. But Tish and Billy Ray don't want their superstar daughter growing up too fast. They asked Miley to live at home until she turned 20. In exchange, they gave Miley her own wing of their California home. Miley's personal space includes a teal-colored bedroom with zebra print chairs, glittery pillows, and a blue throw rug. Her dressing room is decorated with hot pink walls and silhouettes of black chandeliers. The room has a black-and-white checked chair and ottoman for seating. It also has a large, gold-framed mirror. On each side of the mirror are six shelves lined with shoes.

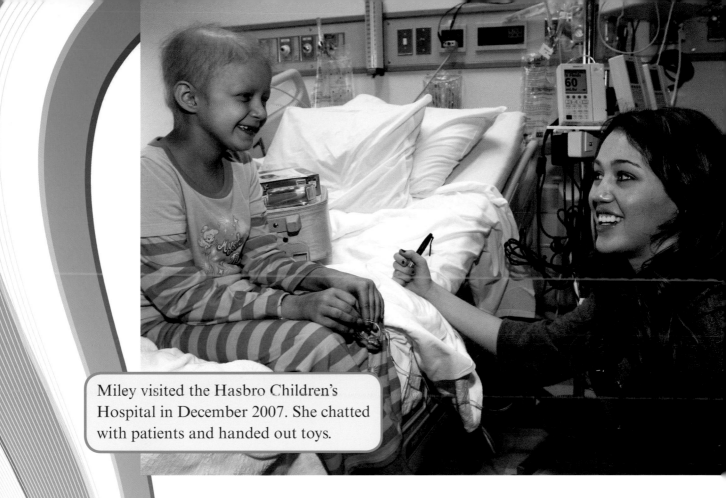

Miley visited the Hasbro Children's Hospital in December 2007. She chatted with patients and handed out toys.

In addition to singing and acting, Miley has other plans for her future. She wants to start a clothing line that is trendy, comfortable, casual, and cute. After high school, she plans to study fashion and photography in London. Miley became a published author when her memoir, *Miles to Go*, hit store shelves in March 2009.

Miley Ray Cyrus has been able to put her singing and acting talents to use, grow as an artist, and help others in a big way. She has grown from a hopeful little girl to successful teen superstar, all in front of a huge audience. Now the world will be watching to see what Miley does next.

Glossary

accomplishment (uh-KOM-plish-muhnt) — something that has been done successfully

agent (AY-juhnt) — someone who helps actors find work

audition (aw-DISH-uhn) — to try out for an acting role

brooch (BROACH) — a piece of jewelry that can be pinned to fabric

chiffon (shih-FON) — a sheer fabric especially of silk

disposition (diss-puh-ZISH-uhn) — a person's general attitude or temperament

imperfection (im-pur-FEK-shun) — the quality of being faulty or not perfect

inspiration (in-spihr-AY-shuhn) — the process of being mentally stimulated to do or feel something

media (MEE-dee-uh) — TV, radio, newspapers, and other communication forms that send out messages to large groups of people

memoir (MEM-wohr) — a narrative composed from personal experience

premiere (pruh-MIHR) — the first public performance of a film, play, or work of music or dance

silhouette (sil-oo-ET) — an outline of something that shows its shape

Read More

Alexander, Lauren. *More Mad for Miley: An Unauthorized Biography*. New York: Price Stern Sloan, 2009.

Jones, Jen. *Becoming a Pop Star*. 10 Things You Need to Know About. Mankato, Minn.: Capstone Press, 2008.

Magid, Jennifer. *Miley Cyrus/Hannah Montana*. Today's Superstars. Entertainment. Pleasantville, N.Y.: Gareth Stevens, 2009.

Tieck, Sarah. *Miley Cyrus*. Big Buddy Biographies. Edina, Minn.: Abdo, 2009.

Internet sites

FactHound offers a safe, fun way to find Internet sites related to this book. All of the sites on FactHound have been researched by our staff.

Here's all you do:

Visit *www.facthound.com*

FactHound will fetch the best sites for you!

Index